Chapter 1

My life as a Falconer.

I received my California Falconry license in 1976, at the age of 16 years old. My first license was issued in Diamond Bar, California. At the time Diamond Bar was a sleepy, hilled Suburb about 25 miles East of Los Angeles. It was also the perfect place for a young Falconer to a take a bird out and hunt, which is the goal of Falconry. The art of Falconry is to take a Bird of Prey and train it to hunt with you, the Falconer, as a partner. Falconry is not pet keeping, and is not solely a blood sport. Anyone who gets a license and has his or her bird, just to have it sitting around is not a Falconer at all, and they are looked down upon by the Falconry community.

The blood sport aspect is real, but it is the end result of hours and training. Falconers are, or should be, Conservationists. Falconers are aware that the prey they take from the wild are a precious commodity, and as a Falconer who hunts the land on a daily basis, sees that other species of predators depend on the same rabbits, or whatever, and are conscious not to over hunt an area, no matter how many animals their bird could catch. In other words, it is not the quantity, but the quality of the successful flights. I have arrived at fields, where for years I took one rabbit a day, and seeing a pile of rabbits rotting in the sun, riddled with shotgun pellets. The worst violators, something that shaped my worldview, were the Earthmovers, and trucks that would show up during my youth and turn a vibrant ecosystem into a dead zone within a couple of days.

Before I had even heard of falconry, I was the type of kid that found interest and wonders in the hills surrounding my home. I would find and bring home Snakes, Tarantulas, and all types of wildlife, show them to my parents, and then release them back into their habitat. I wondered at the Red Tail Hawks that I saw flying around my neighborhood.

I soon took an interest in Pigeons, and my parents let me build a Coop for them in the backyard. This held my interest until I saw a man with a hawk on his fist at the age of 15. That was the first time I had heard the word Falconry, and I knew at that point I would become a Falconer as well. From that day on, Falconry, and learning all about it was what I thought most about. If you are like me, and after that first exposure, you knew you wanted to be a Falconer; it's a blessing and a curse. If you are hit hard by it, you will make it part of your life and you will blow off girlfriends, gatherings, and even Thanksgiving, if you have a hawk or falcon that NEEDS to get flown.

I had heard there was another kid in my High School, named Ken, who was as interested in Falconry as much as I was. We soon met and became fast friends. All of our free time was dedicated to either finding and climbing hawk or owl nest, and locating any books on the subject. The books we tracked down were the older English classics that can still be found today, and we spent hours learning the specific terminology of Falconry, the methods of training hawks and falcons, and making or acquiring all of the necessary "Furniture," or equipment necessary to own a falcon or hawk. We also learned that we could get our licenses, after taking a test issued by the California Fish and Game.

It wasn't like today, when you can, at the click of a computer mouse find hundreds, if not thousands of links regarding Falconry. We had to do it the hard way, and most of our knowledge at the time was based on old books written by people thousands of miles away, and practiced falconry in a strict traditional style. Falconry has changed by leaps and bounds since I first started flying, and the rules and methods have changed as well. I'm not going to try and reinvent the wheel here, as a new Falconry enthusiast can find out anything you want to know about Falconry right there at the computer. I would like to share my experiences, what I would have done differently, the things that have worked for me, and to point out that as long as you have a healthy, happy bird that is getting flown regularly, there is really nothing you can do wrong. I've also included lots of pictures that show how I have modified traditional methods of doing things that work for me. They may not be how others like to do things, but these are the things that I have developed the make my life easier, and also my birds.

The old idea that hawks need to be flown on "Fur," meaning rabbits, and that falcons need to be flown only on "feather," or birds isn't necessarily how you have to do it. Additionally, the European tradition of flying a falcon from a "waiting on," a thousand feet over your head position might not be possible for you where you live. I have watched Harris Hawks flown on ducks from the fist, resulting in amazing, sporting and challenging flights. I have seen GyrPeregrine Hybrids flown on Jackrabbits, again with spectacular results. I have also seen falcons flown from the fist at ducks in an urban drainage ditch. "Car Hawking," something that is illegal in some states, has taken off for the urban hawker, and I have seen YouTube video's of Kestrels catching Starlings right out the window, in exciting, twisting and turning flight. The point is, is that if you have a bird that is healthy, happy, and you have provided your bird the opportunity to catch game, there isn't much you can do wrong, so experiment.

I've flown and released a Great Horned Owl, and a Screech Owl, both given to me as a kid, as the people that found them knew I knew how to take care of them. I've flown several Kestrels that my friend and I trapped before I received my license, they were both released. My first real hunting bird was a Tiercel Red Tail that was given to me as a confiscated bird from the Fish & Game Dept, through my Sponsor. I flew an imprint Female Red tail that I found and legally took from a nest. (I will explain why that is legal and beneficial later.) I was given in 1984, one of the first Captive Bred Harris Hawks in California. I have been given, or purchased at least a dozen other Harris's over the years. I have flown two Tiercel Chamber Raised Captive Bred Peregrines. In California I flew an Imprint Captive Bred Gyr/Peregrine. In Montana, I flew Two Female Imprint Gyr/Peregrines, that were raised and flown together, (That was amazing.) I think that's it.

Over the years, I have purchased items that I knew I couldn't make, like Hoods, Scales, and Swivels. I bought my first real Falconer's glove, and bag from the famous glove maker, Kalem, in his garage in San Gabriel Ca. I have also made a lot of my own furniture to suit my purposes, and they still work best for me. I have experienced closeness to nature that really can't be replicated. I have made many mistakes, but I have only had one bird die one me. It wasn't my fault though, it was my first Gyr/Peregrine, and she crashed into the ground after hitting a duck off a pond at about 100 MPH. It was a great flight, and she just couldn't pull up. One thing that has never happened to me, and I would have a hard time living with it. I have never had a bird die due to a mistake I made. I have been close, but it just never happened. If you choose to be a Falconer make sure it does not happen to you.

The following is some information for the average person, and not necessarily a Falconer. During your life, you may come upon, or know someone who finds a baby hawk or falcon that has fallen out of a nest. Of course, you want to contact the proper authorities who can pick up and rehabilitate this bird. However, it may be some time before they can get to you.

If the bird is not yet able to fly, you need to put it in a safe container, and get some food into it. I would suggest a large cardboard box, with towels on the bottom. As far as food goes, don't feed it hamburger or anything like that. Go to a pet store and buy some rats or mice. If you are squeamish let someone else do the food preparation. I know it sounds cruel, but again life feeds on life. The easiest way to kill a mouse or rat is to grab it by the tail, and throw it at a wall in the garage. I know how awful this sounds, but it kills them quickly, and whatever bird you found needs to eat. After it is dead, remove the intestines, and chop up the mouse, fur, bones and everything. That is how they are fed, and they get the calcium. Once it is chopped up put it in front of the bird. If it is a while since it has eaten, it will probably eat it right up. If it doesn't recognize it as food, take a small chunk, and put it in front of its face. If it opens up its mouth in fear just drop it in. They will most likely get the point and eat. Make sure you contact the right people, be it a Rehabber, the Fish & Game or whoever, and give it to them. Enough said about rescuing a bird.

Chapter 2

Owls, and getting my license.

When I was turned on to Falconry, I found out what was necessary to get a Falconry license, the written test and getting a Sponsor. It was about a one year process, between the ages of 15 and 16. At 15, I had been hooked, and I found a friend that was just as eager as I was about Falconry, and we collected every book we can find. I was still living at my parent's house, and they were very supportive. I had obtained a list of what falconry equipment was necessary to have before I could attempt to obtain my license, and I also found a list of other falconers with licenses, and even heard about the two falconry clubs. These were the CHC, or California Hawking Club, and NAFA, the North American Falconers Association. I was also advised that a Dept. of Fish and Game Warden had to come out and inspect my "Mews," or hawk house, and sign off that it was adequate.

While I was going about organizing my falconry "Furniture," or equipment, a couple of neighborhood kids came by with a baby Great Horned Owl in a pillow case, and told me that they had found it in the hills. They said that they knew that I knew how to take care of it, so they brought it to me. Of course I wanted it, it was possible that they had found it on the ground, because I knew that Great Horned Owls typically bail out of the nest when they are still unable to fly, and when their eyes are still blue in color, and are fed by their parents on the ground. I saw the eyes of the Owl were still blue, and that it was basically blind, and this is the only time they could be tamed by people. With that little bit of information, and the 10 dollars they wanted for it, I took it even though I knew that legally I wasn't supposed to have a bird yet, but I knew it would probably die if I didn't take it.

With that, I had my first bird, Tecolote, Owl in Spanish. I knew enough at this point how to raise a young bird, chopped up rats, chopped up birds, chopped up snakes, feeding everything, including the bones, fur and feathers. I knew that they need the calcium from the bones, and I knew that they would digest the meat and regurgitate the bones and the feathers in the form of a pellet every day, called a "Casting." I raised my owl in the backyard, in the falconry method, and taught him how to fly to my fist for a piece of meat, just like the books said. Soon he was fully grown, and had the run of the back yard; I was basically using a technique called "Hacking," where a bird is allowed to fly free on your property.

Soon, I had a full grown Owl living in my yard, my "Mews," made out of a shed was built, and I had all of my equipment ready for inspection. Also, someone had dropped off a Screech Owl that was also living in the trees of the yard. I had studied all the test material provided by the Fish & Game, and I was looking for a licensed falconer to sponsor me, or teach me how to really be a falconer. I started calling all of the names on the list, and finally found a sponsor who lived in LA to help me.

This is when things started to get interesting for me. I met my sponsor, Mike, a "Master" falconer, and drove to his house every week to flying with him. Mike was a great sponsor, and best of all he had 3 Harris Hawks he was flying on rabbits. I had never seen a Harris Hawk before, because they don't live in California. Harris Hawks, at the time, I believe in the late 1970's were still nesting on the California side of the Colorado River bordering Arizona. Falconers were allowed to harvest Harris's on the California side, I might be wrong. But somehow California falconers were getting Harris's legally. Again, I may be wrong, but quite a few falconers a generation older than me were getting them. I had ne idea what a bird could do until I saw Mike's Harris's hunt bunnies and Jacks. They made Red Tails look like they were standing still.

Through mike I was introduced to Telemetry, which is a transmitter you put on your bird in case it is lost, as well as the benefits of having you birds wear a well fitting hood. Some people like to use transport boxes like converted dog kennels, but I personally like the control of the hood.

I ordered a metal bow perch, covered it with Astroturf, bough an "Ohaus Triple Beam scale, and made a triple to Mr. Kalem's house to buy a real falconer's glove and bag, at the time it was what you had to have. I guess you can call it a little bit of history I was involved in, a personal visit to the famous Kalem garage, where I also bought "Sampo" swivels, which attach to the leash of your bird.

I don't know how I did it, but I was studying for a test, building a Mew, going out to fly Mike's Harris's weekly, and I still had time to learn and trap Kestrel's, further developing my falconry skills. Kestrel's, were fun. They are true falcons, and on the list of birds an "Apprentice" falconer, as I was soon to be, was allowed to keep. They were fun, we would trap them, train them to fly to our fists, and eventually release them. The idea of using them to hunt birds like sparrows and starlings never came to me, and as I was not even driving then, using them to "Car Hawk," was not even a question. In my mind, getting a Red Tail, which was allowed to an Apprentice, and then getting a Harris Hawk after I graduated to a General was my goal. Licensing was a matter of time. You become an Apprentice, after two years you became a General, and after 3 years you became a Master.

Eventually, the time came to take the falconry test, a multiple choice question test that included a little bit of history about falconry, identification of birds of prey, how to care and recognize disease, and identification of falconry equipment. I had no problems, my sponsor signed off, and then a Fish & Game Warden came out to inspect my facilities. This was a bit stressful, as I had to make sure there was no evidence of birds being there before I obtained my license. The Warden came out, briefly inspected my stuff, complained that the concrete in my Mews was sloppy, but signed off on it anyway. If he would have looked closely, he would have seen a Great Horned Owl asleep in the back yard tree and a Screech Owl in one of the bushes. Interestingly, the Great Horn lived in the back yard tree for several years, and eventually brought home a mate. The Warden pet my dog Tigger, and checked her license discretely as he left. With that I paid $17 and received my apprentice license.

Chapter 3

My First Red Tail

Shortly after receiving my Apprentice License, I began making traps for an immature Red Tail hawk. The regulations stated that you may only possess one bird until you are signed off by your sponsor that you have learned enough to be granted a General License after two years. During the apprenticeship you may only capture an immature Red Tail hawk, or a Kestrel. You may not take an Eyas, which means a bird from a nest. Some people are against falconry, because it depletes wild birds. In actuality, it helps the survival rate. Numerous studies have been done, the conclusion being that there is an 80% mortality rate for birds of prey their first year. This can be due to many factors, mostly predation and starvation.

The reasoning behind allowing falconers to take first year birds is two fold. Trapping an immature Red Tail for instance, and you can tell they are immature because they do not yet have a red tail, you pretty much insure that the one you trap will survive much better than in the wild. Also, taking a young bird for a nest that has more than two young increases the chances of survival for the remaining birds, as the competition for food has been reduced. This can be debated forever.

I didn't have to go through all the trapping, as I received a phone call from my sponsor saying that he had an immature male Red Tail that had been confiscated, and asked if I wanted it. I didn't ask what condition it was in, and said yes. What I received was a perfectly mannered bird with not a broken feather. When I picked him up, he had already been fitted with "Alymeri" Jesses, which are just anklets that attach to the hawk's Tarsi, or leg. He was sitting on a Bow Perch when I picked him up. I had manufactured a car perch, tied him to it, and he rode home in the station wagon I was driving at the time. I had lucked out with my first bird.

As I said, I am not going to reinvent the wheel here and go over training methods, explain terminology; there are great Beginners Falconry books out there, I suggest you read them. Falconry like everything else is evolving, and I do things differently than I did 40 years ago. I don't buy expensive gloves anymore, and I build my own perches. Some things I leave to the professionals, things like bells and hoods. Let me just say though, I find Pakistani Bells to be the best, and I like Dutch Hoods. I still remember being excited when my first bells came in the mail, and I attached one bell to my bird's leg using a simple button Bewit.

Flying to the fist is still flying to the fist, and that is what I did with this bird. I flew him every day, rain or shine. I adapted my scale with a perch, just a piece of 2x4, and checked his weight every day. The deal is you want a hungry responsive hawk. You do not want a starved hawk, you are training an athlete. Within a week, he was flying free to me, and per my sponsor's suggestion started hunting rabbits with my dog Tigger, as she knew how to find rabbits, and just need to work as a team with the new bird. I didn't have far to go. Right down the street where a High School stands were my hunting grounds, lots of bushes, hills, and Cottontail rabbits.

I also joined the California Hawking Club, and started going to meeting. My advice to those of you interested in falconry, join a club and start meeting people. There weren't too many people my age, all the active falconers were about 20 years old or more, and they all seemed to have a Harris. Anyone that wasn't hunting was pushing for captive breeding laws, as the Harris Hawk in California was now off limits. But the people that had them, along with Peregrines were pushing for breeding rights.

One thing people need to realize is that this was a time when the Peregrine Falcon was all but extinct on the West Coast. Those that had Peregrines in California were teaming up with Universities, and starting breeding projects. From what I witnessed, and have continued to believe, it is because of falconers that any captive breeding and release projects have succeeded. Over the years, falconers that I know have become prolific breeders and we can thank their hard work for bringing Peregrines back in California, and making captive bred Harris Hawks available to all licensed falconers.

If you are new to this, get to know people, falconers. They can be secretive and cliquish, especially here in Southern California, where it is getting harder and harder to find places to fly. Trying to get someone to show you where they fly their birds is difficult; at least it was for me. Everyone was older and it took me a while to find the kind of people I like to go out and fly with. Sure, there are groups that meet every weekend, even out here, but places to fly are becoming more difficult to find.

I was lucky in my introduction, no one was hunting in the Diamond Bar area, and I had the whole, what was to become a High School, to myself. Once I had my bird flying free, we hawked every day. The only thing I can suggest about being a good falconer and catching game with a Red Tail, is getting your bird strong by flying to the fist, start kicking bushes, and get your dog in there. Hold your bird high over your head, kick the bushes, and sooner or later a rabbit will run out. Once your bird sees that, they will chase.

Some catch on faster than others, and weight control is a major factor when getting a new bird to catch game.

    Now you can, and I suggest getting a good digital scale, really get the flying weight right. When I started it was the Triple Beam, and it was Grams. If you are flying every day with a Red Tail, that bird is getting stronger, and putting on muscle, and losing fat at the same time. Throw in what you are feeding, be it Quail, baby chicks, or washed meat, and the outside temperature, and you are faced with many variables on whether you will be successful or not.

    Experiment with weight, and if your bird is chasing hard, it will either catch a rabbit, or grab some fur. The difference can be a Gram, on whether or not your bird id fully committed. Once you start getting fur you are close, and don't be discouraged. It took about a month of hawking every day until my bird caught his first Bunny. After that he began to catch rabbits on a regular basis. If you have seen Harris Hawks hunt, don't try to compare your Red Tail with a Harris, although they are Buteo's, a Red Tail just can't do what a Harris can.

    I was very happy with a rabbit every other day. I was lucky in that I never had to use a "bagged" rabbit, (or a domestic one that looks real,) I don't like having to do that. However, with your first bird, and if he or she is becoming discouraged, you might have to do it. When you do, make a big deal of it, and set it up like a real hunt. Let your bird eat until it can't take another bite.

I was also lucky with my first bird, as I never had to use a Hood, I think Hoods are a great tool, but with my first bird, he rode around in the car bare headed, and was mellow all the time. Another important point, be it a Passage, or Eyas, expose your bird to everything from the beginning, Horses, dogs, kids, anything that might spook it down the road. Additionally, do all of your training, be it flying to the fist, or giving the Lure, (which should be seen by your bird as a full meal when it's produced,) out doors. Your new bird may be flying to your fist in the living room when it sees it, but outdoors you have to start all over. Avoid this by starting outdoors, I found the best place to be on a deserted Football field, at 6AM, when there is no one around.

I took 30 rabbits my first season, and it was a lot of hard work but it paid off. The next two seasons I began flying different locations, with different terrain. After two years of successful hawking, my bird started soaring around with a Female Red Tail near a local college. There was lots of game there, and he would soar on the Thermals with this other bird for hours. At 19, having discovered girls, the commitments of college, and being on the wrestling team, I reluctantly cut of my bird's jesses, and released him at a ridiculously high weight, in the hills were we hawked, and I went to school.

I would catch glimpses of my bird from time to time when I went running in the hills; he had paired up with the local female. I tried to tell my wrestling teammates, as we ran through the hills that that used to be my bird I was pointing at. I don't know if they believed me, but I didn't care. It sounds like a Fairytales ending, but it was true.

Chapter 4

An Eyas, and a Passage Red Tail

I took a couple of years off from falconry, got married, had a kid, and got hired by LAPD. By 1982, I was going stir-crazy to get back into Falconry. I wanted a Harris Hawk, and I started to get to know some of the breeders who were becoming successful. In the meantime, as a General Falconer, I decided to get a Passage Female Red Tail. I started getting my traps together, and tried to explain to my wife just how obsessive I would become about flying every day if I were to get a bird. She said she was cool with it, and helped me prepare.

On the first day of trapping season, equipped with harnessed pigeons and Bal-chatri traps, and rats, we began driving around looking for suitable birds. My Son, Chris, in his Baby-Seat, was also along for the ride. For several days we saw nothing but males. Too keep my wife interested, and to assure her I knew what I was doing, we sacrificed a couple pigeons, and caught two Tiercel Redtail's. My wife wanted to be the one to run out and grab the trapped birds, but she had no idea the damage that can be done by those feet, so I told her no. A bit of advice, make sure you grab the feet! A lot of people use glove for this, but I have always felt more confident using my bare hands, and I have never been footed. Both the birds, which were fat and healthy, were released, having first eaten an easy meal, as I wasn't too concerned if they weren't tangled or not.

The next day we headed out of Diamond Bar, which was invaded by Construction Companies. The fields were being bulldozed faster than I had ever seen. Diamond Bar's "Country Living," was a thing of the past. We were part of it as well, as we had purchased a Condo there. I hadn't built a Mews, but that is a point of contention with me.

I understand that an Apprentice needs to learn how to build a proper Hawk House, but today falconers are living in Apartments, and getting by just fine with a Wall Perch or whatever. The regulations that a Master Falconer maintains a Mew are ridicules. If a falconer can keep a bird healthy, make sure it can't hurt itself, and has access to a bath, those laws need to be taken off the books.

I had made a Bow Perch out of PVC pipe, with outdoor carpeting surrounding it in my garage for the time being, in preparation for my new Passage Red Tail. I would soon find out it was not adequate for a Passage bird. But I am getting ahead of myself.

The day we went out trapping, we found nothing out in the Eastern areas from Diamond Bar, which were at the time Grape Vineyards. We were on our way back home, and in a construction area two miles from our Condo, I spotted a huge Female Red Tail sitting on a Telephone Pole. I threw out a Harnessed Pigeon, and she was on it as soon as I threw it out the window. Five minutes later she was eating it not 25 feet from our car in a grated field. I waited for the telltale signs for her being tangled in the nooses of the harness, and as she stepped away from her completed meal, the harnessed pigeon moved with her. She was snared. I jumped out of the car, she saw me, and took off, only to be held back by the nooses, and the two pound weight at the end of the nylon string.

I was able to chase her down, and as soon as she realized she was caught, she was on her back, with Talons ready to grab. As I said, I like to grab the feet. Some people throw a towel over the bird, but that gives them time to struggle and get free. I have seen it before. I grabbed both feet before she could grab me, and when she realized she was immobilized she went into a state of shock, mouth open, and just frozen, they all do.

The next order of business was to get her hooded, banded with the Fish & Game, zip-tie band, and into the car. Good Hoods are hard to make, and I have always left that to the people who know how to build good one. I like Dutch Hoods, and there are several places to buy them. If you don't have a hood that fits well, your bird will always hate it, and you are off to a bad start. This was the biggest Red Tail I had ever seen, she was fat, and her feet were scared from catching Squirrels.

Once we got her into the car, the next thing was to put on her Alymeri Cuffs, Jesses, Swivel and Leash. Being around Falconer's, I have learned that the best Leather to make jesses from is Kangaroo, it can be found, don't skimp on this. The Eyelet I use for all my bird's Jesse Cuffs is a two piece brass eyelet that is secured with modified Vice-grip pliers, which quickly secure the cuff. A little bit of history. Alymeri Jesses were invented by a Falconer named Guy Alymer. His design, which is now a legal requirement for Jesses, was published in 1971. Before this, Jesses were one piece of a leather strap that dangled from a bird's legs. Birds regularly died when the Jesse became tangled.

As for the Jesse that goes through the Eyelet, today, people use all sort of material. Some use Nylon, Dacron, and you can buy a complete set up just about anywhere. I still like kangaroo. The swivel I use is a Sampo, they never fail. I also make my own leashes from a method my sponsor taught me, a button type, with braided nylon. As for securing a new Passage bird to a perch, make sure you have a clip on your glove, and don't release it until your bird is securely tied to the perch. Birds will Bate, (attempt to fly,) at any time, and the worst case scenario is your freshly trapped bird flying off with Jesse's, swivel, and a leash. That will be a dead bird. Although you might want a fancy glove for your first bird, my Kalem glove was wore out, and I have found gloves that work just fine from Home Depot. For a Passage Female Red Tail you will want something thick, as she will try to hurt you through your glove in the beginning.

Once we got home with my first Passage Red Tail the work began. I spent hours and hours of getting her to stand on my fist, and even more hours getting her to accept the Hood. She wouldn't eat for three days, this is typical, and getting her to sit on the Bow Perch in the garage was impossible. She was just too strong, and was going to hurt herself, or ruin her perfect plumage if I allowed her to keep throwing herself off the perch.

Necessity is the mother of all invention, and I needed a perch that I could use for the car, for keeping this monster secured and uninjured. I came up with the following that I still use today. It holds several birds, its portable, there is no way for them to hurt themselves, or damage their plumage. I thought about a Screen Perch, but they are dangerous, in that many a falconer has found their bird hanging dead from it.

I've included a picture of what I consider the best all around perch, for me. This is how I made it. I want a fairly heavy base, so I started with a piece of ¾ inch plywood. It's rectangular, about 4 feet by 2 feet. I center a 4 foot 2x4 down the middle, and I secure it with L Brackets, and bolts. The top piece the birds sit on is another 4 foot 2x4 and I secure that on top of the other 2x4 with rectangle brackets, and bolts. I don't have the top 2x4 sitting directly on top of the other 2x4 however; I create about a 1 inch gap before securing the brackets on each side of the 2x4s. On top of this I cover the top 2x4 with the thick style Astroturf used for floor mats. This makes a fairly heavy perch that I tie my birds to up to the swivel. That is the purpose for the space in between. I center the swivel on the leash, tie an over hand knot, and tie the leash securely to the perch, making sure the swivel is on top.

The way I have this set up is that up to three birds can sit on this, and unhooded, when they bate, the length of the Jesse allows them to land on the platform with their feet, but not too far that their tail comes over the top of the perch and gets tangled. Additionally, when a new skittish bird is Bating, they don't build up the momentum that they would on a bow perch, and injure themselves. This perch can be used for anything. For this passage bird, when I placed it up on a table, she quickly became content and accepted it, being up higher. It's also heavy enough that she couldn't move it. Make sure when you are putting it together, you space the 2x4's so that your bird's tail clears the platform. The heavier turf also prevents foot problems, and is easy to clean.

Training this bird was a difficult task, I had to really bring her weight down before she started to come around, accept the hood, and allow me to touch her. I started taking her out to fields after the second week, and the perch was great for training. By the end of the first month she was flying fifty yards on the Creance. Important point on the Creance, and especially a Passage Red Tail that has a lot of power, don't attach the end to something that doesn't move. Use weights, as they inevitably try to make a break for it, and can break a leg unless their momentum is slowed down.

Eventually, I was flying her free, but she was always on the wild side. I started hawking out in Ontario, where there were a lot of Jack Rabbits, and other Falconers with Harris Hawks. I was disappointed, as this bird just wanted to hunt Squirrels, and we were seeing a lot of Jacks. She would put in a halfhearted chase, but would break off at the last moment, or grab fur. I knew the issue was weight, but I had already brought her down a lot, and I didn't want to bring her down any more. Thinking about it now, I wouldn't want to grab a Jack Rabbit that was twice my size. However, I didn't want to fly the dirty Squirrels we had here. They aren't like a rabbit; they bite, and fight back.

I stayed with the bird for the whole season, she never really tamed, but being wild, she always had a bit of fear in her. That made for great traits in the field, she never Footed, which some Imprint birds will do. I didn't have telemetry, as losing her would not have been a big deal. Eventually, the season ended, and my bird dropped a Deck feather on her tail. It was time to say goodbye. I started to gradually bring her weight up, and continued to take her out. After a couple days, she was catching thermals in the same remaining hills at the same local college I released my first bird. In fact, she had been trapped not a mile from there.

When she was at a weight where she was almost in a wild state, I took her out to the hills, and cut away her Jesses. With a look, I cast her off for the last time. She made a straight line toward a pair of Redtail's slowly working the thermals. She made the first sound I had ever heard since I had had her, an unmistakable begging for food sound directed toward the circling pair. It's not too much of a stretch to think that one of the circling adults was my first bird, and this was one of the offspring, the Geography was right.

At work, I heard there was another police officer that worked for Vernon PD, just east of my area that was also a falconer. On patrol, I made a trip over there and introduced myself to Tony, who was in fact a falconer, and lived further east in Chino. We too became fast friends, and began to hang out. He liked to go to bars as much as I did at the time, but for purposes of this book, I will keep to the falconry aspect of our friendship, which would include 10 years, a few Harris Hawks, Cooper's Hawks, and some amazing flights. Tony is a bit of a loner, like me, and we had similar ways of flying. We tended to avoid the falconry groups; maybe they avoided us, as we were both cops, now that I think about it.

The idea that Fish & Game Wardens consider, or considered most falconers, in the early years of falconry, semi-criminal, or at least persons to be weary of was brought to my attention, when a Warden appeared at my house in the summer of 1984. He was surprised that I was a police officer, and gave me his opinion of falconers, as well as captive breeders. He believed Falconers regularly hunted out of season, and that captive breeding was impossible. It was believed that breeders were regularly raiding falcon and Harris Hawk nests, and presenting them as Captive bred. (This ridicules assumption on the part of Law Enforcement has been debunked. Thousands of falcons and hawks have been bred in captivity.)

The Warden told me he was at my house for a surprise Mew inspection. I didn't have a Mew, or a bird, but since I was a cop, the idea of any inspection of my property was dropped. Interestingly, when you receive your license, you sign away your Constitutional Rights. You agree that you will allow any Fish & Game Officer to inspect your facilities at any reasonable hour. The Warden said he did have a problem. He said he had just confiscated a young Redtail Hawk nearby, and wanted to know if I would rehabilitate it. I said ok, with the promise of building a Mew at a future date.

With that, I now had a half grown female Redtail that I said I would rehabilitate. Rehabilitating is not really falconry, but it was something to do while I waited around for a captive bred Harris. To make a long story short, the Red Tail was eating on its own, and didn't seem to be imprinted on humans. I made sure I wasn't associated with the food I fed her, and soon I was trapping mice for her to find in bushes, giving her domestic rabbits that looked wild, and she was catching squirrels. Eventually, I released her and she was never heard from again. She was released with a numbered band, and she was never heard from.

Chapter 5

Female Harris Hawk

1984 was a busy year, Tony and I were looking for Harris Hawk breeders, and I had met another falconer named Bob Zepke. Bob was a master with Coopers Hawks, and was flying an Immature Harris, captive bred. These were the first birds with the Seamless metal bands that identified them as captive. I started hawking with Bob, and showed me what they were really capable of. We went out to massive area surrounding area of March Air Force base. Bob liked to take me because I was a cop, and the MP's allowed us to hunt on the property.

MAFB was loaded with Jack Rabbits, and Bob's Harris would see a Jack about 300 yards out, and she would be on, gaining altitude, and working her way over the jack and doing a wing over maneuver, and slamming it right in the head, as opposed to the body, in which case she would get bucked off if she didn't walk up it's back and lock onto the head. Harris's needed to learn this trick, as Jacks used their hind legs to devastating effects.

When his bird was on a Jack, we had to run and make sure she had it secured and was in control. Bob, as most falconers, would dispatch the rabbit quickly, as they would scream. When you hear a rabbit scream when a bird crashes a bush you know your bird got it. It is thrilling to hear, but you want to put it out of its misery quickly, and sometimes you could get here quickly enough and trade the rabbit with your bird for a piece of meat you have on your glove. Harris will do that all the time, its not ripping your bird off of a well earned meal; it is just exchanging one for the other.

The differences between a Redtail and a Harris are day and night. Harris's will fly together with other Harris's, as they live in groups in the wild. They will crawl through bushes, and they will grab Jack Rabbits that weigh as much as 12 pounds due to their group hunting instincts. That's why we had to run after Bob's bird all the time, we had to get there to make sure she had it under control. A 36 ounce Harris Hawk like Bob's, did a good job, controlling Jacks by grabbing their head, but they could get hurt. Over the years, I have seen tiny Male Harris's that weighted 20 ounce tackle Jacks with no fear, and learn to lock up the head, and wait for the falconer to arrive. This is due to that group hunting instinct. At Falconry Meets, I had seen up to 10 Harris's flying together, it is something you have to se to believe.

I continued going out with Bob, bringing my son Chris out with me quite a bit of the time. He loved it and got to see nature, and the struggle of life and death up close. I wanted him to se the beauty of the chase, not just the kill, and the saw the will to survive in all of the rabbits we hunted. Sure, Harris's can catch 300 rabbits a year, where a Redtail may catch 60. But a good number of rabbit managed to evade their way out of death. If a catch was a sure thing, nobody would want to do it, I certainly wouldn't. That is why I was drawn to Falconry. Doing your best to provide an opportunity for you bird to be successful was all you could do. The rest was up to them. I made sure my Son learned that and there was nothing malicious in the way a bird killed. I need to eat, and you are food, nothing cleaner in the whole world.

As the summer was approaching, getting my first Harris was all that I could think about, and Bob introduced me to a breeder named Lance Stump who was breeding Harris hawks, as well as falcons. I called hem, told him I was interested in a Harris, and he invited me and my family out to his house in Hemet for a meeting. Susie, myself, and Chris went out to Lances house, and made our introductions. His commitment to breeding birds was evident when he arrived. He had built a huge facility that he was planning to breed Peregrines in. The breeding chambers were larger than his house, which was a Mobile Home at the time.

Susie didn't hate Falconry yet, and Chris liked seeing all the birds. The Harris Breeding Chamber was out behind the Falcons chambers. He walked us to chamber, and I was amazed. Inside was a pair of Harris's, a huge nest that contained two baby Harris Hawks, a male and a female. The Female adult was huge, and was irritated by our presence. Lance told me that the Female was Penelope, a bird that used to belong to a Falconer I had known, but I don't remember his name. The babies were about 15 days old, and were beginning to show the differentiations, the female the larger of the two. I was drawn to the female, thinking of the Jack's I would hunt.

Once inside the house, I was told that there was another Falconer interested in the female. Falconry regulations were in limbo at the time, and selling captive bred birds was not yet approved. Lance said that he was short on food, and would give the Harris to the falconer that donated the most pigeons to his project. With that a plan was formulating in my head, and I told him I would do what I could.

Once home, I began scouting out locations where pigeons roosted at night and approached the owners of those locations, and asked if I could remove the birds. They were all wild, or "commies," and a nuisance. All of the owners gave me permission to remove the birds, and with the help of my wife, and my young son, the hunting began. We would go out every night with my pellets gun, and shoot pigeons. Susie was delighted, and helped collect the pigeons that I popped. Soon we had 200 gutted and plucked pigeons.

I called Lance and told him what I had. He was overjoyed, and said the bird was mine. He said there was a slight problem, and that I would have to come out the next weekend and get her, as Penelope had laid another egg. The bird was only 8 or 9 weeks old, which is a bad thing with Harris Hawks, as you want them to remain with their parents at least for 12 weeks, when their feathers are fully grown in, and they are totally imprinted on the parents, meaning that they know they are a Harris Hawk. You don't want a Harris that will imprint on a human, as that can cause problems later when you are flying with other Harris's.

Harris Hawks that have remained with the parents for over 12 weeks have been taught to respect the adult plumage of an adult, which is different. A Harris that has imprinted to a human doesn't respect other Harris Hawks, can become a "Screamer," at home. They won't have a natural fear of humans, and can form bad habits, like screaming, but they might also become aggressive over food, and "foot," or grab a falconer when they catch prey in the field.

I didn't have a choice, it was either pass or take the bird as is. I had just built a Mew in the back yard of the house, and I wasn't going to pass up this opportunity. When I picked her up, she was fully feathered, but she still had about 4 inches of her tail to grow out before she was ready to fly. It was easy to bring her home. Lance went in the chamber, grabbed her around the body and placed her in my car on the perch I had developed. She stood up, and being in shock from being removed from the only location she had ever known, rode home without moving.

I placed her in the Mew at home, which had a 2x4 Astroturf perch, a higher shelf perch in back, and she could see out the front, which was vertical PVC pipes, spaced about 4 inches apart. It was a good mew, and because she couldn't yet she was mellow inside. Normally, you wouldn't allow a new chamber raised bird to be free in a Mew, as a Harris taken at the proper 12 plus weeks would fly around and hurt itself.

I had some plans on how to disassociate me with the presence of food. I spent a lot of time with her in the Mew, just me or Chris sitting inside the 8 foot, 8 foot, 6 foot Hawk House, while she got accustomed to our presence. At feeding time, I would drop a Quail or a Baby chick through a hole in the back on to the shelf perch. She got the idea that food just appeared, and ate without us around. For food, and you can get this anywhere, I purchased 1000 frozen baby Cockerel day old chicks, and 1000 frozen grown Quail.

    She grew quickly, and ate all that I put in there, as she could pull food apart by herself. Chris was going on four, and he spent a lot of time in the Mew, and started calling her Maid Marion. She now had a name. When she wasn't eating I introduced her to the glove, and the Hood. I didn't try to put the hood on, simply let it be in her presence. As she tamed, I spent time touching her, stroking her, and touching her feet. When her tail was almost grown out, she was used to the mew, and would allow me to put the hood over her head. I didn't Strike the Braces, just put it on and took it off. I also put on Alymeri Cuffs, jesses, and one Pakistani Bell, using a leather Bewit. She spent a few day picking at her jesses, but accepted them. Soon I was able to Strike or close the Hood, and she had no problem with it. She would simply fall asleep if I left her alone. This is the importance of a well fitting Dutch Hood. Some like Arab Hoods, I like Dutch.

When her feathers became Hard-penned, or when the blood is gone, and they are hollow, I introduced her to the Bow Perch in the back yard, and always had her bath pan nearby. The Perch was covered with the same green floor mate thick Astroturf, which covered all of her perches, and she learned how far she could go being tied to the perch. The bell is invaluable, as you can tell from the sound exactly what is going on outside on the perch from the sound of the bell. We began going out to fields, and I fed her on my glove, which was something new. I exposed her to everything I could think of, even walking around Horse Stables. I did this while I fed her.

At home, I started weighing her every day, and I could tell by the feel of her Keel that she was very fat, and she had little muscle. This had to change, and I started flying her to the fist for tidbits. Bob was still around, and he was getting his female back into shape, and we met at Bonelli Park, know as Puddingstone Lake at the time. The property around the lake was, and still is loaded with Cottontails. It also has a lot of hill, Cactus, Rattlesnakes, and Poison Oak. Only one other Falconer I know flies there, Charlie Cogger, and he has had great success there.

When Bob and I met in the field, I was still flying Marion with a Creance, as I was concerned about loosing her. Bob was flying his bird free and we spent a lot of time together allowing the birds to get to know one another. His bird was in Adult plumage, something my bird should have respected. She didn't, and was initially aggressive when we put both of the birds down on the ground together. This didn't last long, as Bob's bird, experienced and strong was having none of that. When my bird raised her Cackle Feathers and tried to be tough, Bob's Harris grabbed my bird, held her to the ground, screamed at her, and that was the end of the aggression.

Bob was read to start hunting with his bird, and I was still flying mine to the fist, her weight was down, she was building muscle, and was coming to the glove instantly. With that, and his impatience, Bob asked me why I was still not flying my bird free. He said, "Where is she going to go, she only knows you?" It was a good point, and I put away the Creance and started hunting with Bob and his bird. A lot of people over the years have asked me the question, "Why doesn't your bird fly away?" I explain that my by bird is a hunting partner, and looks to me to provide food. I kick a bush long enough, and a rabbit will come out, the bird wants to be there for that.

With Marion now free, and me slightly concerned, we started Hawking. I didn't have Telemetry at the time. I should have, but a lot of "Hawker's" didn't use it. The people that flew Falcons on the other hand, they all had it, and used it. There are two types of Falconers, Hawkers that get into the dirt and bush with their birds, and those that fly Falcons. They look for spots to hunt ducks, and in my area, that meant Golf Courses, and they flew their Falcons high in the sky. I hadn't been introduced to this yet. But I had heard that it was a cliquish group that kept the locations of their hunting ponds secret, and barely tolerated new people in their training fields. I wasn't worried about that scene yet, but I would in the future.

In the field with Bob and his Harris, I picked up on some of his traits, and use them today. In the field, Bob removed the Jesses from the Alymeri cuff, and didn't use flying Jesses. As you don't want your bird being hung up from the slit in the normal Jesses that attach to a Swivel and leash, they replace the Jesse strap with a Jesse that has no slit and cannot get hung up. They then can hold on to their bird if they want to keep it on the fist by grabbing the Jesse strap. Harris Hawks are smart, and although they will fly to your fist for a tidbit, if you make a habit of holding on to their Jesses, they will never return to the fist as a hunting platform. They will think you are going to secure them.

This whole issue disappears if you remove the Jesse from the cuff and never hold your bird tight. If you are hunting in an area where Bunnies will get kicked up at your feet, your bird will quickly learn to stay on the fist, as to not miss an opportunity for a Bunny that goes from a bush to a hole.

Marion's introduction to Hawking was easy, as she watched as Bob's bird chased rabbits, and in no time at all she was following Bob's bird. That's the way young birds learn in the wild, and I was lucky to have another Harris there as a "Make Hawk." However, Marion was quick to realize that all she had to do was follow Bob's bird, look like she was putting in an effort, and get a reward from the catch. Although she was catching on over time, she was never taking the lead. I needed some alone time to get her to catch.

The very next day, in a little field that was left in Diamond Bar, Marion caught her first Bunny. I couldn't be happier. From then on she was a bunny machine. I didn't really have to bring her weight down that much, and we would take a bunny a day, sometimes the first rabbit that flushed was caught. I could have tried multiples, but I wanted her last thought of the day to be that she was a badass and could catch rabbits, and get a full crop for the effort.

When flying bunnies, which are flights that are much closer than Jacks, you really want to stop that rabbit from screaming, although you loved to hear the initial scream. My preferred method of dispatching a bunny was to grab the head, where my bird's feet were holding on, grab the hind legs, and do a full Chiropractic. This would completely sever the spinal chord, and end the suffering. If I was close enough, and the bunny had just been caught, I could sometimes get there and release it unharmed.

The trick to this is to approach your bird, holding a nice open piece of meat, and get her to step on the glove, and let go of the rabbit. You wanted a nice clean step off, and not a tugging match, and you want to make sure the first 100 rabbits you catch end up with a full Crop for the bird. The thing about hawks is that they don't have a particular kill method for their prey. They do know to go for the head, and then they begin eating. There have been a couple of times that my bird caught a rabbit in a Thicket. When I got to her, she had only grabbed the rabbit by the hind quarter, and had eaten what was in front of her; the rabbit was still alive hidden by the brush. This has also happen when she caught a rabbit going into a hole; she just started eating the leg. They have no sense of dead or alive, just incapacitated and eatable, or not. Then they adjust to make it eatable.

Harris Hawks do best when they grab the head. They also like the brain, which is very high in calories. Some Falconers use a knife to open the skull for the hawk. I discovered a better way. Simply crush the skull with your gloved hand and pull the ears apart. That opens the brain cavity, and they can get to it readily. If you don't want your bird gaining too much weight, get as much fur into it as possible. I give them the ears, face, and any other fur you can. It will come out as a Casting the next day. On the first rabbits, I stuffed by Harris to where her Crop was the size of a Tennis Ball.

You can either let your bird eat on the ground while you replace the Jesses, swivel and leash, or you can lift her to the fist and put it on that way. Once she is done, she would begin "Feaking," or cleaning her Mandible on my finger or my glove. After that the hood goes on and we walk back to the car. That is my argument with the hood. If you are far away from the car, you have to make sure your bird is busy eating on the way back. If she finishes her meal before you are back to the car, you have a bird that wants to be any place but there, and it is a hassle keeping it on your glove. The hood does away with all of that.

After about 100 Bunnies, it was time to fly Jacks. We started at March AFB, where Jacks were everywhere. It was a long drive, but this was my drug, and we had to hunt. The transition to Jacks was easier than I anticipated. I never restrained her on the glove, and she would follow along from any high perch she could find. You can always tell what a Harris is chasing from the way she takes off from a perch. A Jack Rabbit flight is a calculated flight, where position is taken before the wing over is made and hopefully a rabbit is caught. A Cottontail is a different pursuit. It is a fast pumping in an attempt to get to it before it gets to cover. They learn to time it just right, just before the hole, amazing.

By the end of the season, Marion had caught about 200 rabbits. Compare that with a Redtail that catches 50 in a good season. For me the Harris is the all around rabbit hawk. Redtail's are good birds, don't get me wrong, but they were just not made to do what a Harris does.

The following year Tony, my other cop friend got a Tiercel Harris and named him Flib. We let the birds get to know each other, and we began to hawk the Air Force Base, as well as the Vineyards of Ontario, that were just getting the attention of the Construction Companies.

Rain or shine, out partying all night, or whatever, we were out hawking when the Sun went up. It took a little while, but flying in a "Cast," the Falconry term became second nature for Marion and Flib. They would work as a team on Jacks. Flib being the smaller male, would fly out, turn a Jack around, and be slammed by Marion. They had teamwork down, and we kept our freezers full. Nothing was wasted, we both had recipes for Cottontail, and the Jacks were used for the summer when the birds were Molting.

We were good stewards of nature, and we never depleted the fields. We did however, on occasion flush a Burrowing Owl from the ground, and one or the other birds would catch it. We would try to get there before it was killed, and it was about 50/50. In the third year, about 1987, we saw the Bulldozers coming. They would make a mockery of our attempts to moderate and alternate our fields. They killed everything in their wake, and our fields began to shrink.

Chapter 6

Peregrine, and two Harris's

In 1988, at a Falconry Meet, Flib was electrocuted, and lost a foot. He tried to fly with us, but he was never the same. Either through Falconry, my job, or just my arrogant youth, my marriage fell apart, and I was living with my Girlfriend in Irvine, an area that still had places to fly. I made sure Chris was still involved in my life In fact; Marion still had a home in her Mew in Diamond Bar. She was going through the Moult, and was scheduled to be part of a Harris Hawk release project.

I wanted a Peregrine. I found a breeder in Wyoming who had a male Peregrine for $1500.00., I bought him. Tony and I made a road trip to Wyoming, having a delightful time in Salt Lake City, which were found to be anything but Pious.

When we arrived, I found my bird hooded, and ready to go. He was one day out of the breeding chamber, having never seen a human. The drive home was a long one, trying to keep the bird calm. One thing I can't stand is a bird with broken feathers. It happens, but you want to make sure you do all you can to keep your bird looking good. It was never a problem with Harris Hawks, their feathers were durable. You could have your Harris looking like hell after a Jack Rabbit battle. Within an hour of being home, a Harris can jump in a bath, Preen, and come out feather perfect. Falcon's feathers are a bit more delicate.

We made it home, and the first order of business was to get Telemetry ordered. When I started using Telemetry in the 80's, the best was a receiver and antennae from Custom Electronics, and a pair of good Telemetry.

Training was slow. Getting him to sit on the fist was a fight. He didn't eat for two days, and he liked to bite. A Harris Hawk's strongest weapons are its feet. A Falcon is different. The bite of a falcon is designed to decapitate birds, and when they bite you, you know it. I did the same thing as with a Harris, I introduced him to things as his Manning progress. Eventually, he took the hood without complaint; he would fly to the fist, and he would fly to the Lure for a complete meal.

Some Falconers use flying to the lure as a sort of game, teaching the bird to pass by a swinging lure, which is amazing to watch, and is a good workout for the bird. I stink at lure flying; I wanted a high flying falcon to catch ducks. I had been out to the field were the falcon guys train. It was an empty area bordered by mountains separated by ten miles, and not a telephone pole in sight. The last thing you want from a falcon is for it to land, and they are attracted to poles. This was the perfect place, and I had watched falcons 1000 feet up in the sky flying overhead. The only giveaway was the sound of a bell overhead. At that point, a pigeon is released, and out of nowhere the falcon stoops on the pigeon. It is breathtaking, if you blink, you miss it. The falcon hits the pigeon, knocking it from the sky, and circling down to claim the meal.

This is the initial training for Duck hawking, when your falcon is ready, you fight for spots to catch ducks in the area, or you take longer trips for other prey. It all depends on the falcon. I wanted my falcon to hunt small ducks. Looking back now, what I went through just to fly, as I mentioned, it is an addiction. When my Peregrine was tame enough to fly to the Lure for a meal, I drove the 80 miles to the training field.

I usually brought someone I knew with me, as other coppers, girlfriends, whoever wanted to go out and watch this. My arrival to the well known training field was met with a lot of sarcasm by the falcon guys that had been flying there for years. That didn't deter me, and it would end up being an adventure. Not that I didn't already have enough on my plate, I had also purchased a Male Harris from a breeder in Louisiana, Dr Neil Smith. The Harris was home waiting to be flown in the evening.

Getting a male peregrine to fly is easy. Getting him to fly high took time. I used the Pigeon method. Some people use a Balloon with a lure attached to get a falcon up, some use a kite, and some use pigeons. Pigeons are great, but it takes time just like everything. It starts like this. In California, when young falcons are being trained, this has to be done at the break of dawn; otherwise it is just too hot.

The first day flying free is the most suspenseful, as you are releasing a barely tame falcon that you have no idea what it will do. You arrive at the spot, and make sure there are no other falconers flying, and you check the sky for Eagles. They love to catch and kill falcons. Keeping your falcon hooded, you slide the perch out and you test you radio transmitters by inserting 372 hearing-aid batteries, and making sure they are giving off a continual beep on the receiver. A transmitter then was a tubular device, as round as a hearing-aid battery, and about an inch long. This had an Antennae extending out of it.

Attach one transmitter to each leg using a plastic zip-tie, through a connector on the transmitter through the eyelet of the Alymeri cuff. If your falcon flies off, you can track your falcon's location using a directional, hand-held Antenna. This is necessary because in the first season you will be using it a lot. Once a falcon learns to really fly, a flock of Pigeons in the next county will attract their attention, and they will go to investigate.

A new falcon is like a blank chalkboard. You want to go from A to Z, which is a steady falcon over your head, there are lots of steps. Once your falcon has the transmitters attached, it is time to prepare your pigeons. Some people use elaborate bags to hold Pigeons, I use camo pants, with lots of pockets. Three pigeons is the standard every day. One pigeon is a strong Homing/Racing Pigeon; even the strongest Peregrine cannot catch a pigeon like this unless they get lucky. The next Pigeon is slightly hampered. Using a piece of electric tape, create a cone behind the eyes, disabling the pigeon from seeing behind it. The last pigeon has tape over its eyes, when thrown up in the air it will only hover. I know this sounds cruel, but Pigeons again are food for your bird, and this is training. You also need to have your lure ready, and garnished with food. Your falcon should already know that the presence of the Lure means food, and to come in.

Now you are ready for your first flight that will probably last a minute. Walk your falcon away from the car, as some pigeons, once they see the falcon will head straight for it. Interestingly, you know that the chances of completing a season with your falcon, the odds are against you. Anything can happen, an Eagle could catch your bird, it could get shot, it could crash, and it could get hit by a car following a flock of pigeons heading for the safety of a Freeway.

None the less, you walk out; remove your bird's Jesses, after attaching on eyelet to a special clip secured to your glove. This is done because falcons know when they are getting ready to be flown, and get impatient. Some will try to fly with their hood on, and you don't want to be the guy who lost his bird that way. When ready, unclip your bird while taking off the hood.

What should happen is this. Your bird should look around a few times, "Rouse" its feathers, "Mute," and fly off you hand. Remember, your bird has never flown before, make these first flights quick. If your bird takes of quick and begins to gain altitude, wait until it is about at its highest point and throw the Pigeon that just hovers. Yell the traditional Falconers, "Ho Ho!" Your bird should turn, fly in and catch the pigeon. Once your bird has caught the Pigeon, it will generally decapitate it and begin eating. Walk slowly up to your bird, and let it keep eating. If you can, and the bird is comfortable with your presence, reach under while it is eating, and secure your falcon. Once things have calmed down, you should be able to present your bird with your glove beside it, and the bird will step up on your glove. That is the day, feed your bird what you think will be the right amount, and like a magician, slowly make the rest of the pigeon disappear. Hood your bird, put it and the pigeons away, and that's your day.

Day after day this is how I trained my Peregrine. Depending on what he did when he left my glove, he received a reward or not. When he was flying up and away, he received an easy pigeon. If he didn't fly higher than the day before, he was either served a pigeon he would chase but could not catch, or the Lure, where he didn't get rewarded much in the field. When he was brought home, depending on his weight, he received enough to sustain him.

Little by little the flight time increased, muscle was built, and he gradually lost fat. After a month, he was up to 300 feet, flying in wide circles, and keeping an Eye on me the whole time. If he set his wings to glide, he would receive the pigeon he could not catch. He would try, but the strong homer would head to the sky, followed by my bird. When he eventually gave up the chase at a much higher level, he would be given a pigeon he could catch.

He began to learn that the higher he went, the easier it was to catch his pigeon. It wasn't as straight forward as that though, I wish. When he learned he could really fly, he would sometimes disappear over the mountain range. This is where telemetry came in. If he would disappear, I would track him, sometimes miles away, where I would throw out the Lure. He would appear out of nowhere, and get a meager reward for at least returning. This is where proper weight management is key, and I tended to fly him too high, I admit it.

At home, he was always restless on a Block perch, bating all the time, just due to his restless instincts. Peregrine is a word that means wanderer, and they do wander if you do not keep the weight just right. It is hard to do, weight management has several factors, the type of food you are feeding, temperature, and the amount of flying time he was getting.

I hated the fact that he bated a lot, and I tried every type of perch I could think of to keep him happy, and he certainly could remain in the Mew free, as he would injure himself. I also knew it was only a matter of time before he hurt himself on the Block perch, or broke a feather. I finally came up with a perch for falcons that they like. It took me a while to design this, walking the isles of Home Depot. I knew he wanted to be up high, so I started there. I found a base, a cement umbrella stand made of concrete. In the center hole, I inserted and secured a metal ½ inch female pipe fitting. On top of that I screwed in a 6 foot, ½ inch pipe, with threads on both ends. On the top I screwed in a female threaded round metal platform, which had mounting hole through it. For the perch on top, I secured a round wooden platform about 10 inches wide. I covered it with my standard, green floor mate Astroturf. In the center, I placed an eye-bolt, for securing just the swivel.

With this perch, my Peregrine sat up high, he had no ability to gain momentum in his bates, as the swivel was secured to the center. It took him a while to adapt to it, but eventually he was able to perch comfortably, with his tail feathers extending out and down the side. He didn't have room to hang himself either, with the length of the Jesses. I was able to place the perch anywhere, even in the living room, to my Girlfriends chagrin.

To add even more torture to my life, I had a fresh Male Harris to fly, and within a month of receiving my Master's license, I took in another male "hand-me down" male Harris, that someone I knew didn't have time to fly. My life was busy, being a police officer until 10 PM was getting in the way of flying three birds. I would get off work, get up at the crack of dawn to fly the Peregrine, Fly both of the Harris Hawks together in what is called a Brace, work out, spend time with Chris, and get to work. This was a time when Girlfriends were at the bottom of the list, and I was bouncing from one to another. Looking back, I had been quite selfish, first with my wife Susie, and a couple of really nice women who didn't deserve to be on the bottom of my "to do" list. Women reading this, if you meet a Falconer, don't get involved. However off topic that seems, it is applicable when writing about my life as a Falconer.

The Peregrine was hard work, he was either two small to see above me, showing some excellent style, or he was off in another County, killing Pigeons on his own. It was a weight problem, I know it now. But it is a fine line, and too low, I didn't want to go there. The two male Harris's were great as a team, and they taught me what two 25 or 28 once birds could do to a 12 pound Jack. If they chased the same rabbit, which they almost always did, they were easy to handle, as I hade picked up an idea for a great hunting perch, from Charlie Cogger, a great Falconer, and a great friend.

The hunting perch was simply a garden rake, the solid one piece type the makes a "T" at the end. I just put a Green Astroturf floor mat over the top of the rake, and held it high. The birds got the idea and sat on that thing as I kicked bushes. When they made a kill together, I pulled the rabbit apart, and let them eat. While they were eating, I attached their Jesses, swivel and leash, which had been tied around my neck. When they were done, they were hooded and tied to the top of the perch while I walked back to the car. The only problem occurred, when they went after different rabbits in opposing directions. I had to find one, and then the other, and get them secured. I had seen Charlie go into the field with six Harris's before, and he was able to do it.

Life was good, in regards to hawking. I had purchased my own house in Rialto, California, which was closer to the rabbits, as well as the field I flew the Peregrine. The only problem was the job; I was driving 60 miles one way to work, and another 40 East to fly the Peregrine. The Peregrine was flying high, and I was about to enter him on Ducks, and the Harris's were doing what they do. Flying fields were becoming parking lots faster than I could keep up with. The area Tony and I flew in Ontario was dead, nothing but housing and building. I was in Ontario recently, in a Park that had once been a wildlife habitat that provided food to eagles, hawks, and Burrowing Owls. To me it was a dead zone. It's hard not to be depressed by those little things.

One day in 1989, my Peregrine disappeared; he never stopped flying long enough to pinpoint his location. I tracked him to the Palm Springs area, and found a dead pigeon where his transmitters told me he was located. There were lots of tree there, and he refused to come in on the Lure, as he had just eaten. I stayed there that night, and by 3 AM, he was off. I tracked him to another half eaten pigeon. This went on for 7 days, until the batteries on his transmitter went dead. He was gone.

It was June, and I was depressed over his loss, but I knew he would survive. The plastic zip-ties would soon break off, and eventually his leather Alymeri Cuffs would rot away. However, I added another Peregrine to the population, which was needed. I was half wild anyway, and only tolerated my presence. I never heard from him, although I still look up his Band number.

The summer Moult was coming up, and I was exhausted. I made a decision with the two Male Harris Hawks; I would release them in areas Harris Hawks historically lived, instead of selling them to other Falconers. Harris Hawks were pretty inexpensive, and I knew these two birds that had been raised by their parent, and were also half wild would be able to make it on their own with that, I phoned the Santa Cruz Predatory Research Group, and asked them where a good place to release them would be. I was advised of an area in the Salton Sea area, which would be perfect for them. With that, I went out to the area, and camped out in an area that had wildlife. For two days, I took them out and hunted. It was loaded with prey, and they killed rabbits, as well as quail, which they had taken occasionally in the field. Feeling good about it, I reassessed them together in the area. They were oblivious to what was going on, they just continued being Harris Hawks.

Chapter 7

GyrPeregrine, Cooper's Hawk and Montana

Hybridizing Gyrfalcons and Peregrines to make Gyrperegrines, was a common thing for breeders. Gyrperegrines are larger than Peregrines, and the Hybrid is a combination of each bird's best qualities, usually. I had seen Hybrids fly; they are just monsters in the sky, and duck machines. I purchased a female GyrPeregrine from Dan Konkel also in Wyoming, and I made a trip up to his house to pick her up. I had a great hood made, and I got her when she was about 15 days old.

Getting her home as a Downy was easy, and from day one she had the run of the house. I fed her by hand, drove her around and exposed her to everything. I even took her to work. She would sit in an open wooden box in the Watch Commander's office, and saw the world from a Police Station point of view. The band on her leg identifying her as Federal merchandise gave her Carte Blanche, and was the most heavily Guarded falcon in the world.

As she grew, I would drive her to the middle of the open desert, and let her perch on the long Astroturf perch I had designed. As she began to fly around, I would release a pigeon, and she would make half hearted attempts to catch it. I was a game for her, and always got fed on the perch at this stage. I had a Dog as well, and he would accompany us into the desert where we would sit for hours. I would read, and she was able to fly as she pleased, and always returned to the top of my truck for food. Soon, she was learning how to use her wings, and would fly for an hour overhead, waiting for a pigeon to be released. This was a type of Hacking that made it all play, and she learned how to use the sky.

When serious training started, she was hooded, weighed, and I trained her with Pigeons, just like I did with my Peregrine. She learned fast, and soon she was Waiting On at over 1500 feet, I couldn't see her, but I could hear her bell as she crisscrossed the sky. I would throw a pigeon, and she would Stoop so hard it was breathtaking. At four months old, she was ready for ducks.

I had stopped weighing her, as she was totally tame, and the transition to ducks was seamless. The only problem was finding good places to fly in Southern California, as all of the old time Duck Hawker's kept their spots secret. However, being a police officer got me into Golf Courses to fly the ducks in their ponds, where others were sneaking in and sometimes cutting fences to gain entry. I admit I hated the constant driving, and sought out other places to fly.

There was a Falconer I had met while working Patrol in LA, named Tom Cantella. Tom is the owner of "Papa Cantella's" sausage. He invited me to come up to his house near Santa Barbara, where he said he would introduce me to his ponds. The area was great, and my falcon would literally bounce ducks to the ground, killing them instantly.

If this wasn't enough, my friend Tony Brill, had pulled two Cooper's Hawks, both females, and we trained them together. To make a long story shot, both females were raised together, and we both used the same techniques to raise the Accipiters. They both turned out differently, however. My bird for some reason took to Quail with ease, while

Tony's bird would attack his face, or anybody else's that was nearby. I didn't like Cooper's that well, they can be temperamental, and broke feathers regularly, which I hated. I ended up giving my bird away, as it was still an Imprint and unafraid of humans. I didn't want to find out by bird ended up hunting Sparrows in front of kids at some open air restaurant, and become a nuisance.

I was killing ducks regularly, but driving 200 miles a day to do it. I was hooked on Gyperegrines, at what 50 ounces, and I wanted to fly a Gyrfalcon that could weigh between 3 or 4 pounds. I had seen pure Gyr's flown, and if I wanted to avoid the high prices of a breeder, I needed to live where you can regularly and legally get them, and that was Montana. In hindsight, looking to leave LAPD for the purposes of Falconry was a bad decision. However, I was looking around at what City in Montana I wanted to work as a police officer. It's said, when you work LAPD, you can go anywhere, once. After a year long search I decided to apply to Great Falls PD, and I started their hiring process, which was basically to prove that I worked for LA.

My plan was to leave when I had 10 years on, and bring my GyrPeregrine with me. Part of that would happen, but I wouldn't be bringing this bird. This bird was steady on ducks, and loved to pound them into the ground at 100 miles an hour. I was going to make the 100 mile drive to Yucca Valley, where I had a great pond no one knew about. However, I was exhausted, and I decided to fly her on this little pond I knew that was an easy kill, but it was in a hole surrounded by steep sides. Looking back, I can see how a four month old falcon though it was Superman, which is what you want them to think. But it's like putting a 10 year old behind the wheel of a Ferrari.

I arrived at the pond, and saw that it had about 5 Mallards on it, and I got excited. I unhooded my bird, and she immediately went up to about 1000 feet, waiting for me to flush the ducks. It was an easy set up, and I went over the side, and the ducks started to reluctantly come off the pond, as they surely saw the falcon. I saw the Stoop, and then she was a blur. The first sound I head was the smack of the duck, followed by another smack, which was my bird crashing into the ground.

The duck was dead, split open wide, and as I approached my bird, I was sure she was going to be dead. She was a trembling mass of broken legs and feathers, but she was conscious. I picked her up, and ran her to the truck. As fast as I could, I drove her to nearby Vet, who specialized in birds.

When I arrived in the waiting room, there was a young couple also waiting to have their bird seen, a Parakeet. The bird was in the lap of the woman, and was lying on top of the towel. I then noticed a sign in the waiting room that said, "All visits, 60 dollars minimum." Looking over at the Parakeet, I could see that it was obviously dead, but they obviously wanted that fact verified by a professional. I didn't want to seem like I was trying to push myself in front of the line, but I saw no reason for this concerned couple to spend $60 bucks just to have death confirmed. I looked over, and I quietly said, "I am an expert, and I can tell you for certain that your bird is dead. Trust me, save the 60 Bucks." The woman started weeping; they talked quietly together, and then left. After they were gone, an assistant appeared, obviously excited about seeing my falcon, escorted by into the back room.

Vets aren't cheap, and if you can't afford to pay for Vet visits occasionally, don't become a Falconer. In the back, I met the Veterinarian, who quickly did an X-ray of my bird. Her Femur was broken, and it was unclear if her back was. Their opinion was to set the break, and see if her ability to coordinate her body came back over time, as she was unable to move anything besides her neck. With that they said her chances of recovery were poor, but take her home, and see what happened. They said that they could keep her there for 100 dollars a night, but the bill was $1600 dollars right now, and they couldn't keep better care than I could.

I returned home, and to my surprise, she was able to eat when I hand fed her. Otherwise, she couldn't move. I made her as comfortable as possible, and hoped for the best. She went downhill fast, and died on the fourth day. I have nothing but praise for this bird, and I did nothing wrong. It was a great flight, and she forgot to pull up. With that I cut the band off, did the required paperwork, and that was it.

Chapter 8

Two Female Gyperegrines, Trapping Gyr's, and a Lot of Ducks.

I decided to move to Great Falls Montana, and I was hired by the Police Department. In Great Falls lives a Falconer of note, Jeff McPartlin. In Falconry circles he is infamous, connected somehow to a Sting called, Operation Falcon," where several Falconers were arrested, Jeff was labeled as a Rat, and I wanted to know what really happened. McPartlin also was a Realtor, and I went though him to by a house. I also ordered another GyrPeregrine from Dan Konkel, that I was planning to get in June on that year. This was February, 1991, and I was a new Copper there.

There were all sorts of rumors about McPartlin, which he had been arrested smuggling Gyr's from Canada and saying they were captive bred. I asked him about it the first time we met, and he denied that ever occurred. His statement was that he was approached by Falconers who wanted to smuggle Gyr's, and he immediately went to the authorities. McPartlin told me that he had boxes of legal documents at his house and invited my to his home to investigate, and come to my own conclusions.

At Jeff's house, I didn't know where to start. He had a room full of legal documents from "Operation Falcon," and in my spare time, I read through them, promising to make an honest attempt to clear his name. To be honest to those that were involved in this thing, I could not make heads or tails of it. Half of it was redacted, informants were all over the place, and in whatever time this all occurred, which was almost a decade; I read nothing that had an initial implication of McPartlin.

I really could not make heads or tails of this whole operation that touched a lot of people. As a police officer, talking to other Wildlife officials in the area, they were of the opinion that "operation Falcon," which extended from Canada to California was the result of some over zealous Wildlife officials that were convinced breeding in captivity was a front for smuggling operations. This has been proven ridicules, as the progeny and Hybrids produced have been enormous in nature and impossible to fake. If McPartlin was an agent on his own doing what he felt was right, then good for him.

McPartlin on his own had a robust breeding project, and for buying a house from him, he promised to give me a female GyrPeregrine in June. So, I had two Hybrid coming as I settled down into my job as a police officer in Great Falls. One thing that I must say about Jeff McPartlin is that he had a natural ability when it came to finding Gyr's in Montana. As part of my welcome to Great Falls, Jeff took me out on a trapping expedition of the surrounding areas. Within 15 miles of Down Town Great Falls, Jeff spotted a Gyr, and we had it trapped in 10 minutes. It was an Adult, so it was immediately released.

Over the next three years, Jeff would arrive at my house periodically with a Passage Gyr he had trapped. I don't know if this was showing off or what, but he could spot and trap Gyr's better than anyone I have ever met. He also had a menagerie of birds at his house that I didn't want to ask about. He had Tundra Peregrines naturally breeding with Gyrfalcons, I saw it myself. Everything was banded, and he almost had a free pass to the number of birds he could possess. One thing I didn't like was the quantity of Passage birds he took from the wild. He told me that he would trap a number, decide which one he wanted to keep, and release the rest. I hope that is true, but I never did like the fact that the Passage birds need to be hooded most of the time. I understand that Gyr's are easily stressed, and are prone to many ailments. The answer to keeping a Passage Gyr healthy is to reduce the stress, and that a hood reduces this. But if keeping a Passage Gyr healthy means that it is hood 22 hours a day, I would rather see them left alone, and I have never owned a Passage Gyrfalcon.

June finally rolled around and I picked up two downy Gyrperegrines. One from Dan Konkel, and one from Jeff McPartlin. They were both about the same age when I got them, and I raised them together. Everything went well, and I raised them just as I did my first GyrPeregrine, except this time I had two birds being raised on top of my truck on the same perch that I had used for years. Additionally, it only took me 10 minutes to find a training area with no Telephone Poles.

I did everything the same, as they learned to fly, and they learned to use their wings by chasing one another in the open skies, and chase a pigeons that I brought with me. They would fly for an hour, disappearing into the sky, and Stoop together after a Homing pigeon. At the end of the day, they would both be called to the perch on the hood of the truck, and receive their final meal. They were also trained to come in to the lure as the final meal. One thing I have learned about Lures, is that anything can be a Lure, as long is it is associated with a good feeding. I have seen Tennis Balls attached to a string used as Lures, use your imagination, save your money for the things you need like good Telemetry.

Eventually, separate training had to be done to get some control. They both took to the hood well, but that is where any resemblance stopped, although they had both been raided the same. The bird produced by McPartlin progressed well using the pigeon method. However, the bird produced by Konkel just sat on my glove and screamed. It is something that just happened, not the breeder, as the first GyrPeregrine from him turned out to be perfect in every way. It had to be the personality, as when I took them out together; once the first bird took off she would follow.

Entering these birds on ducks was easy, and there were 100's of places to go. It eventually worked out that if I wanted to catch ducks with a high flying falcon, I would have to fly the one that wasn't "Fist Bound." However, If I wanted to watch an aerial display of ducks being chased across the sky and being caught 1000 feet up, I would walk to the edge of a pond, unhood the birds, flush the ducks, and off they would go, sometimes working as a team, and sometimes going after separate ducks. This is how I understand birds are trained for Arab Falconers. I just called it a free for all, and always brought extra people out, mostly other cops, who would help me collect my birds. They would sometimes be found miles from the initial pond, always with a duck.

Great Falls also had Hungarian Partridges, or "Huns." I would hunt the birds separately, as only the one would wait on. The other bird would sit on the fist, Mantling, and screaming until the Huns flushed. She would catch about 50% of the time, and this ended quickly, as she would "Carry," as well, trying to eat the little Partridge before I could get to her. I might have done something wrong, but I can't think of anything I did differently. Just two personalities, I think there was just something wrong with the one's personality. However, they could both catch ducks.

I flew them both for two years, and we caught a lot of ducks. I learned how to prepare many different duck dishes, point being if you are catching game, and you are enjoying yourself, you are a successful Falconer. After three years in Montana, I was getting bored with the job, and with Falconry. My son Chris was visiting during the summer, but that wasn't being a father. My initial plan was to have him living with me; however his mother wasn't going to allow that. It was time to go home.

Chapter 9

Back to LA and beyond

My only option to be a present father was to return to LA, and my old job. That turned out to be harder than expected, with LAPD needing my presence there to redo all of the testing. I was told that my chances of getting back would be easier if I was a resident. With that, I sold my house, gave the two falcons away to local Falconer's, and headed back. When I returned, it wasn't had to get a police job with a local LA agency; I also had enough money to buy another house.

As a Falconer, I didn't want to live in the city, so I purchased some Apartments and a couple houses in Yucca Valley, a Desert area about 80 miles East of LA. For some reason my girlfriend at the time Doni, and her two kids Tony and Cory, decided to drop everything and follow me to LA. I restored all of the Apartments, the houses, and I ended up having a fairly good income generated by renting the properties. I kept one to myself, a house on a hill surrounded by open Desert, Jackrabbits, Cottontails, Ducks and Quail. This was perfect habitat for Harris Hawks, as well as falcons.

My first purchase was a female Harris from a breeder in Louisiana, named Neil Smith. This bird was huge, easily the largest Harris I had ever seen. She was flown in, chamber raised, and had been with her parents a long time. When I got her she was, as Neil would say, "wild as a snake," which is a good thing. I also purchased a male Harris from Bill Murphy, a California breeder, and this bird had also spent a great deal of time with its parents.

My experience had shown me over the years that captive bred Harris Hawks turn out the best when they have remained with their parents for as long as possible. This really solidifies in their brain that they are in fact Harris Hawks, and retain that identity for their entire life. This is imprinting at its best, and the Adults have plenty of time to teach them respect for their elders. These birds will never scream, or Foot, which can be painful and dangerous. I had seen human imprint Harris Hawks in the past, and they are very limited. They can't fly with other Harris's, because they try to kill them, they Foot, and they scream.

    Some Falconers insist on a certain strain or family of Harris Hawks, and the prices are set much higher by a breeder's name. This has not been my experience, and I won't mention any names. If you insist on getting a Harris Hawk from so and so for 800 Dollars, or whatever the price might be, that is your choice. But in my experience, a chamber raised Harris that has been with the parents well past the age of the 8 weeks, when they are hard-penned, will turn out the best if trained right. Baby Harris's are expensive to feed, and some breeders want to get them sold and gone right when they are hard-penned. For a bird that you are going to going to go out and fly with other Harris's, try to stretch out the time they remain with their parents. If it cost a little more to get the breeder to allow your bird to remain with the parents for 20 weeks, you will probably be happier for it.

I built a Mew in the garage, and made a PVC pipe separation for my birds, as soon as they were tame enough to fly free in the mew. This takes a little longer with the older birds, but the hood, and the Long-perch I have made for years settles them down quickly. In the Mew, free but separated when their weight has been brought down is the way to go if you want to develop a team. Never place them in one mew together, free when they are at hunting weight, as the female will kill and eat the male.

As soon as they were flying to the fist, we were out hawking. Introduction to the Astroturf covered rake was easy, and they learned to sit patiently for whatever I kicked out at my feet. Within a week, they were catching bunnies, and that same month they both caught a full gowned Jack.

The flights were amazing, and Tony and Cory were eager to go out. Chris was a bit older and into other things, but occasionally we would come out. Talking to Chris now, he is glad I exposed him to falconry, and he has stories from when he was a kid, in a backpack, out hawking. Tony and Corey were the next in line to see nature up close.

I could write for hours about what a Cast of Harris Hawks can do, but I won't. Suffice to say, we caught everything that was out there, they even came upon Rattlesnakes, which I recommend avoiding. The best flights were of the male, turning a huge Jack, to be smacked by the Female, which had built up so much momentum that the Jack was knocked unconscious. The male would then come in to assist. Separating the two, reattaching the Jesses was easy, and we were back, both hooded, and riding on the T Perch.

Quail were also amazing to watch, the male again rounding up the flock, grabbing a quail for himself, and making it possible for the female to catch one as well. The natural teamwork is amazing, and something that can't be taught by a human. The most amazing quail flights were when each bird was able to catch one in each foot. It happened, I was there. In some cases the male would fly backwards, something I had heard about but never seen.

Over the years, these two birds also learned to use the Thermals of the Desert to reach tremendous highs, followed by a join vertical stoop on a Jack that never saw it coming. As I have witnessed, as far as versatility, there is no equal to a Harris. Sure, a Goshawk can chase faster, but with all the headaches that come along with Accipiters, I choose Harris Hawks.

As the Harris Hawks were a perfect hunting pair, I had time for another bird. I wanted a Peregrine, as I had never really been successful. Bill Murphy was breeding Brookei Peregrines, reputed to be quite tame. I think it was the summer of 1996, when I bought one from Bill, while the Harris's were Moulting.

Brookei's, it turned out, were as easy to Mann and train as advertised. Within two months she was flying higher than any falcon I had ever had and was as tame as a kitten, the complete opposite from my other Peregrines.

My idea was to enter her at Pheasant, as I knew a place. Her first day up over a Pheasant, she smacked it right out of the air. We caught Pheasant almost every day, and as winter came, she transferred her talents to all the duck ponds I could find in the Yucca Valley area, I even came into the City to show her off once. We even went to a couple meets, but I am really not that social, and tended to fly with the same people I always flew with.

My time with this falcon was limited however, and I lost her toward the end of her first season. I don't know what happened, one minute the Telemetry told me she was over my head, and the next, she was gone. Either, both transmitters failed, or she left the area so fast, that I couldn't get a signal. I even rented an airplane to try to track her down, but she was gone.

During this time I had also got a little side business going. I obtained an Agent who booked me to do High School Assemblies all over California and Arizona. It was fun for about a year. I had gotten into restoring Volkswagen Buses, and I took the birds from Las Vegas, to Phoenix, to I don't even remember where. I did 45 minute shows, flying the Harris's around a Gymnasium for 400 dollars a show. The only problem with this is that it took the joy out of Falconry for me. I did it for two years, and after that I was exhausted.

After four years, the two birds were getting "Broody," during the summer, and wanted to breed. I had the time, but I didn't want to be a breeder. That didn't stop the desire in these two birds, and I had a plan. There is an area on the California side of the Colorado River that I wanted to conduct an experiment. I had seen Harris's there before, and I knew that they had once thrived there.

I was quite a Gypsy at the time, and I drove out to the Colorado River with the Harris Hawks. I set up camp, and started hawking with my pair of Harris's that were now a pair. They were fat, and most of the day was spent with them chasing one another. The nights were spent in the bus, with them on the long perch. They could come and go as they chose, and were up catching some kind of Pack-Rat at dawn.

Seeing they were adapting to the area, and they were Copulating during the day, I cut off the telemetry and Jesse Cuffs, and let them be. They stayed in the area, and no other Harris's came in to claim the territory, which was a concern. After the third day, I left, with them sitting together on a Transformer that had been adapted as not to electrocute birds, which had been a problem.

Chapter 10

The Sailboat and reconnecting with friends.

Owning rental property in Yucca Valley ended up being like pulling teeth when it came to collecting rent. For the most part people refused paying rent, even though they were receiving Government checks. The tenants also took great pleasure in destroying the homes they were provided? After the Millennium, the apartments were at a loss. I sold all but two houses, one Doni decided to keep, the other, I still don't know where the deed is? Sufficient too say, I am not a businessman, and had no desire to fight with tenants that had all of the rights.

On my own again, I had the money to buy a sailboat, which I took to the tip of Baja, and back, I settled for a while in Ensenada, took a tour of Europe for 3 months, and I visited Cuba. I was a bit burned out of Falconry, although I kept my license current.

I eventually ended up in San Pedro, Ca, the main harbor of LA. The hills around the harbor had many promising bunny areas, so I bought a female Harris from Bill Murphy. I trained the bird right there on the boat, on my Astroturf covered long-perch. For a couple years, I hawked the surrounding hills, and caught many a rabbit. I had also reacquainted myself with Charlie Cogger who was breeding Harris Hawks, and my old friend Ken from my teenage falconry days.

Charlie was still flying his birds at Bonelli Park, and Ken was hunting Crows with a Harris Hawk from his car window. Ken and I briefly started a business, doing the same Assemblies, and he had acquired an Eagle Owl. The business never got off the ground, and Ken I believe got married.

I still had my Harris Hawk in 2009, and on a whim, drove out to Ontario to see what was left of the Grape Vineyards. It was a most depressing sight to me, as every square inch had been developed. Most see it as a beautiful bedroom community. I can see that, but to me it was a dead zone, complete habitats, extinct. There were some Falconers out there, hunting rabbits in the hedges surrounding warehouses, but that isn't what I would call Falconry. However, it is an adaptation of Falconry, using what is available.

Prologue

My Thoughts

A couple years later, I added my Harris to the small Colony I established on the Colorado River. They are still there; in an area that I am probably the only one who knows exists. As I sit here writing at 56 years old, I reflect on my life, and it has been directed by Falconry. I am sure I will get another Harris, but not this year.

Falconry is an addiction, but if you have that Gene, there is probably nothing you can do but go with it. Have fun with Falconry, and don't be afraid to adapt to things that work for you. When I first started, I had to have that Kalem glove, and I did it a certain way because that is how I was told to do it. Sure, listen to your Sponsor but don't be afraid to adapt.

When I started, telemetry was a bulky and untrustworthy method to recover your bird. However, it was all that was out there. If not today, then tomorrow, telemetry will be a Microchip in your bird, and an app on your Iphone. When I started, falcons had to Wait On at 1000 feet, or you weren't doing it right. I learned that you can adapt to your situation, and your bird, and hunt ducks from the fist if you want to. You can even fly a GyrPeregrine on Jacks, something I would have never thought of doing.

If I were to get a bird today, I know my limitations, and I probably would only get a Harris. I have no desire to chase a falcon 100 miles in the initial training. The equipment I would use would be completely different than I would have used 30 years ago. I have adapted, and I know what works for me and what doesn't.

The reason I wrote this book was to throw in a few tidbits that some new Falconer might find useful, maybe answer some question that they couldn't find in a Traditional Falconry book. I also wrote this because I know Falconers love to read books with lots of pictures. When I started out I read everything I could get my hands on, which wasn't much. Today, everyone is writing a book, and still the new falconers want more. So, here you go, a little more, and I hope you get something out of it. I also suggest the non-falconer's partner, girlfriend, boyfriend, whatever, read this book, just to realize and understand just the type of person they are involved with, or are planning to get involved with.

I want to thank the Falconers that I have known over the years, and who have added to my Falconry knowledge. I would especially like to thank the Falconers that became breeders, in a time when captive breeding was questioned as even feasible. These dedicated people have given their lives to captive breeding, and have made it possible for me to view wild Peregrines from my window. These same people pushed for the sales of captive birds, which are very expensive and time consuming to produce. Of these people, I would like to personally thank Dr. Neil Smith, Bill Murphy, Charlie Cogger, Lance Stump, Pete Widner, Dan Konkel, Steve Baptiste, Dave Jaimeson, and the Santo Cruz Predatory Research Group. If it were not for these individuals, organizations, and many others I don't personally know, captive breeding, Harris Hawks in California, Peregrines, and possibly Falconry would not exist at all.

Good luck, I hope you enjoyed it, Steve